Our Place in Space

Contents

Hello fellow aliens! What do you want to know about planet Earth?

Our Place in Space

Hiya, I'm Zeek.

Hi, I'm Finn.

Calling all aliens!

Are you planning a holiday to planet Earth?

Finn and Zeek are here to help.

'Our Place in Space'
Published by MAVERICK ARTS PUBLISHING LTD

Studio 11, City Business Centre, 6 Brighton Road,
Horsham, West Sussex, RH13 5BB, +44 (0)1403 256941
© Maverick Arts Publishing Limited August 2019

A CIP catalogue record for this book is available at the British Library.

ISBN 978-1-84886-476-4

Maverick
publishing
www.maverickbooks.co.uk

Credits:
Finn & Zeek illustrations by Jake McDonald, Bright Illustration Agency
Cover: Jake McDonald/Bright, Digital Media Pro/Shutterstock
Inside: Images courtesy of NASA
Shutterstock: Vector Tradition (6)

White

This book is rated as: White Band (Guided Reading)

INCOMING MESSAGE

Dear Finn and Zeek,

I want to visit Earth but I'm having some trouble finding my way there. The solar system has so many planets and moons!

Please can you explain the solar system so I can find Earth?

From,
Zoomy
(Planet Faraway)

Introduction

The solar system is the **planetary system** that humans live in. It is one of over 2,500 in **the Milky Way**. There are still more to discover: space is huge!

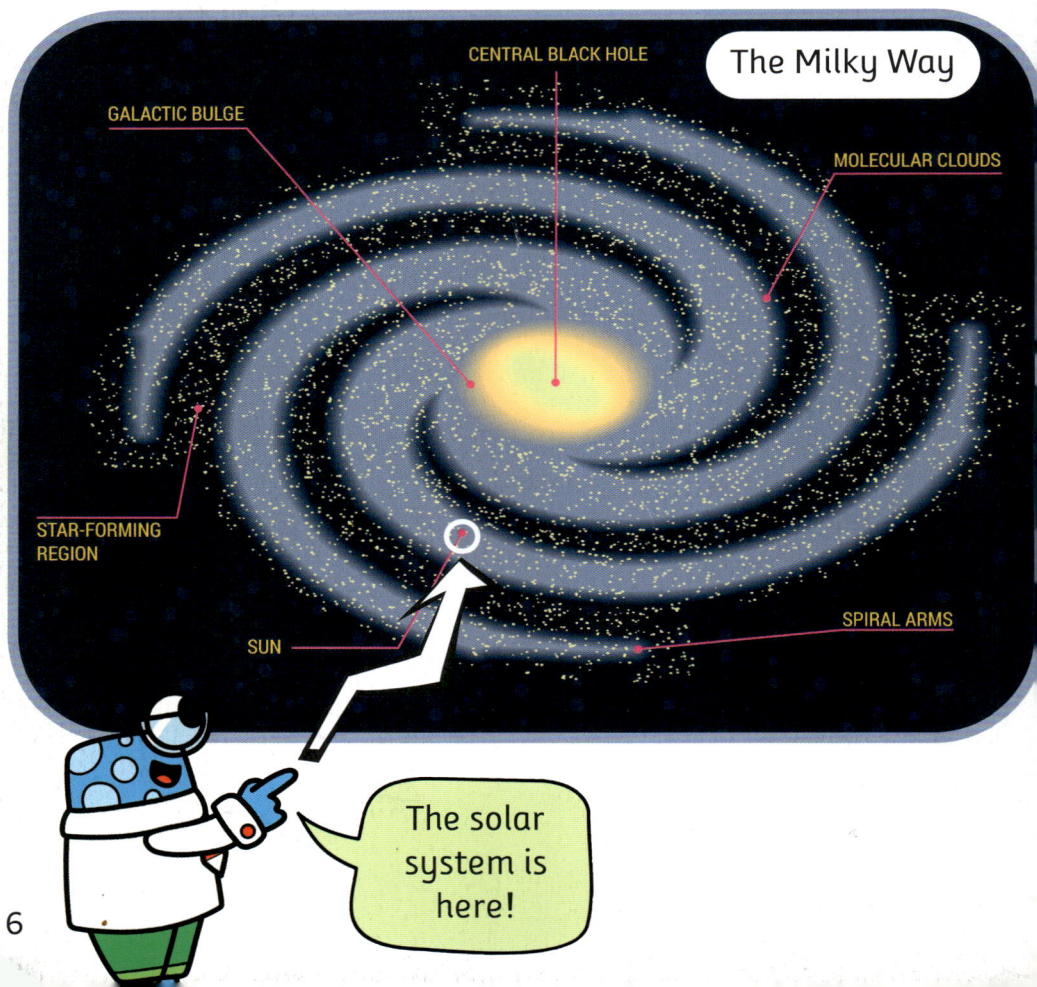

The Milky Way

CENTRAL BLACK HOLE

GALACTIC BULGE

MOLECULAR CLOUDS

STAR-FORMING REGION

SPIRAL ARMS

SUN

The solar system is here!

THE SUN

MERCURY

VENUS

THE MOON

EARTH

MARS

ASTEROID BELT

The solar system has eight planets and five **dwarf planets**, with 193 known **moons**. There could be even more!

JUPITER

SATURN

URANUS

NEPTUNE

PLUTO (DWARF PLANET)

The Sun

The Sun is known as a **dwarf star** and is a sphere of super-heated gas. It releases lots of heat and light! We see it in the sky during the day, but not at night.

The Sun is 109 times bigger than Earth and much heavier!

The Sun is the star at the centre of the solar system. The Sun is so massive and has such strong **gravity** that the planets **orbit** it even when they're really far away.

THE SUN

Some planets have stronger gravity than others. You would feel very heavy if you visited them!

The terrestrial planets are the four planets closest to the Sun, which have solid, rocky surfaces.

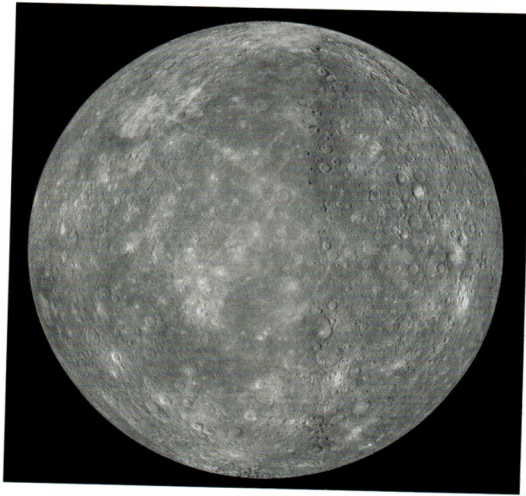

Mercury

Mercury is the planet closest to the Sun and is also the smallest in the solar system. It gets very hot in the day but very cold at night, ranging from about -180°C to 430°C! It takes just under 88 days to orbit the Sun, which is very fast!

Venus

Beneath the clouds

Venus is the second planet from the Sun and the hottest planet in the solar system, with an average temperature of 462°C! The surface is covered with thick clouds. It takes almost 225 days to orbit the Sun. Venus is strange because it rotates in the opposite direction to most other planets!

Earth

The Moon

Earth is the only known planet in the solar system to have life. It's the third planet from the Sun and one orbit takes 365 days (one year).

Earth has one moon. Most scientists think the Moon was formed around 4.5 billion years ago, when another planet, called Theia, collided with Earth.

The Earth is also special for being in the "Goldilocks Zone", a special distance from the Sun which is just right for liquid water. Not too hot and not too cold, just right for life!

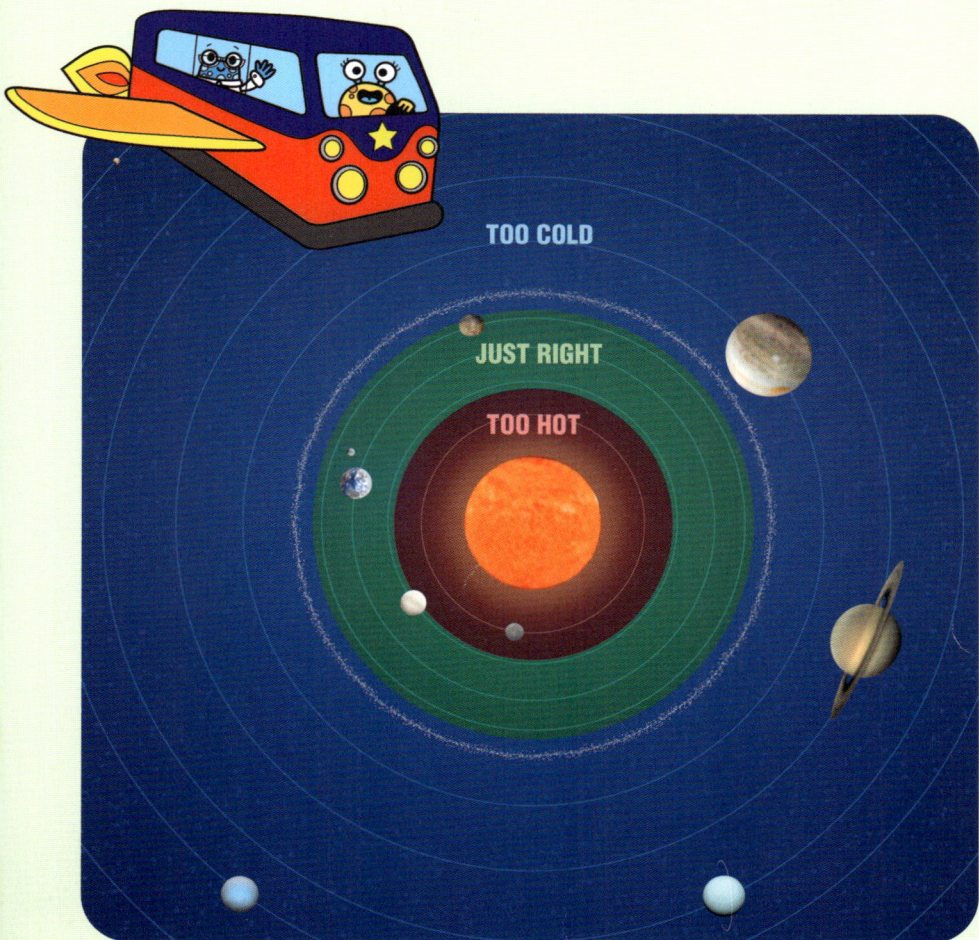

TOO COLD

JUST RIGHT

TOO HOT

Mars is also known as 'The Red Planet', and it's the fourth planet from the Sun. It looks red because its soil contains iron oxide, which is red in colour.

Mars is cold, with temperatures ranging from around -143°C to 35°C. Frozen water has been found on the planet. Mars has two moons, called Phobos and Deimos. Mars is also home to Olympus Mons, the biggest volcano in the entire solar system!

The Asteroid Belt

The asteroid belt is a ring of thousands of asteroids between Mars and Jupiter. Asteroids are made from bits of metal and rocky material. There is one dwarf planet in the asteroid belt called Ceres.

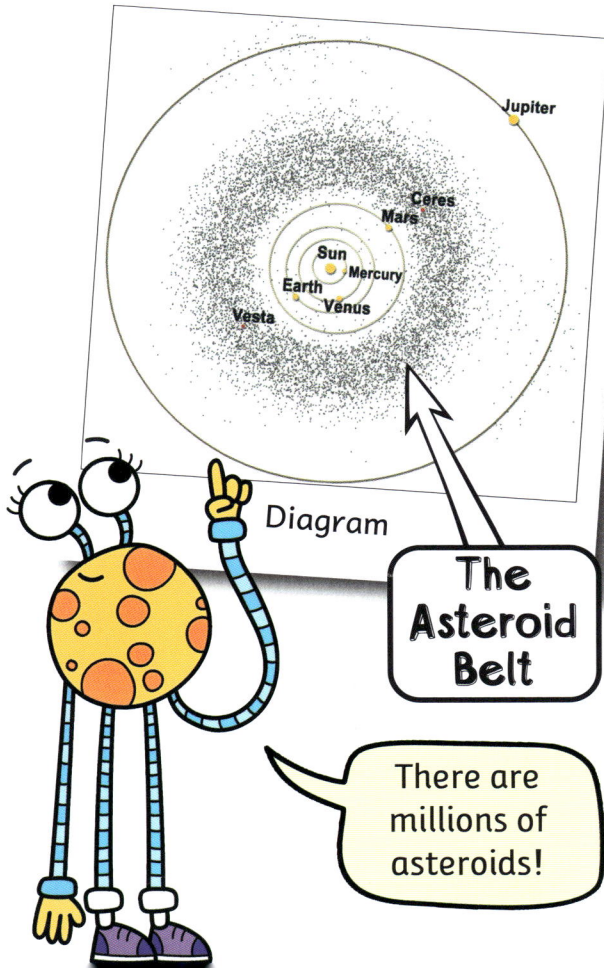

Diagram

The Asteroid Belt

Ceres – dwarf planet

Vesta – brightest asteroid from Earth

There are millions of asteroids!

Gas Giants   Jupiter

Gas giants are made mostly of gas, so you wouldn't be able to stand on the surface! They are thought to have a small, solid core.

The Great Red Spot

Jupiter is the biggest planet in the solar system. The surface of Jupiter always changes because all of the gases are swirling around really fast. One of its most famous features is the Great Red Spot, which is a storm larger than the size of the whole Earth!

So far, 79 moons of Jupiter have been discovered! Jupiter's gravity is so strong that it causes some moons to stretch, making them get very hot, like Io, a very volcanic moon!

The largest moons of Jupiter are called the Galilean moons. These are Io, Europa, Ganymede and Callisto. Ganymede is the largest moon in the whole solar system!

The Great Red Spot has been shrinking since it was discovered. Some scientists think it will disappear one day!

Saturn

Saturn is a smaller gas giant than Jupiter, but still the second largest planet in the solar system. Saturn's north and south poles have huge storms. The one at the north pole is shaped like a hexagon!

Saturn's best-known feature is its rings,
which are mostly made of small bits of ice,
rock and dust. It has at least 62 moons;
the largest is called Titan.

Ice Giants   Uranus

Ice giants are very similar to gas giants, but they also have a lot of ice, made from water.

Uranus is extremely cold, with a minimum temperature of around –224°C!

Uranus has 27 known moons and 13 rings, but the rings are smaller and harder to see compared to Saturn's. The outside of the planet is made of water, ammonia and the methane ice crystals that make it look pale blue. Uranus is very strange because it rotates on its side!

It's the wrong way up!

Neptune

Neptune is the furthest known planet in the solar system. It takes almost 165 years for it to make one trip around the Sun! It has 14 known moons and looks blue.

This is the closest photo humans have for Neptune's true colour.

Neptune has very faint rings!

Neptune is very windy! Even if you could stand on Neptune, the wind would blow you away! Even though it is much further from the Sun, it's roughly as cold as Uranus.

Woah! The wind is dangerously fast!

Pluto

That bit looks like a heart!

Beyond the Solar System

Voyager 1 was launched by **NASA** in 1977, and on 25 August 2012 it became the first spacecraft to travel beyond the solar system. It carries a golden disk with greetings from Earth and information about the human race, just in case it comes into contact with **alien** life.

Pluto used to be known as the ninth planet of the solar system, but it does not have enough gravity, so it has now been renamed a dwarf planet. Pluto is further from the Sun than Neptune and has five known moons. It's very small and very far away. One trip around the Sun takes Pluto about 248 years!

Good luck Voyager 1!

Preparing the golden disk

That's how Zeek and I discovered Earth!

MESSAGE SENT

Dear Zoomy,

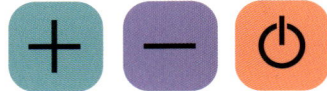

The solar system has eight major planets. To find Earth, look for the biggest planet (Jupiter) then go through the asteroid belt, past the red planet (Mars) and then you should see Earth! It's the third planet from the Sun.

Look out for **satellites** and the International Space Station orbiting Earth!

From,
Finn and Zeek x

Satellite with an astronaut

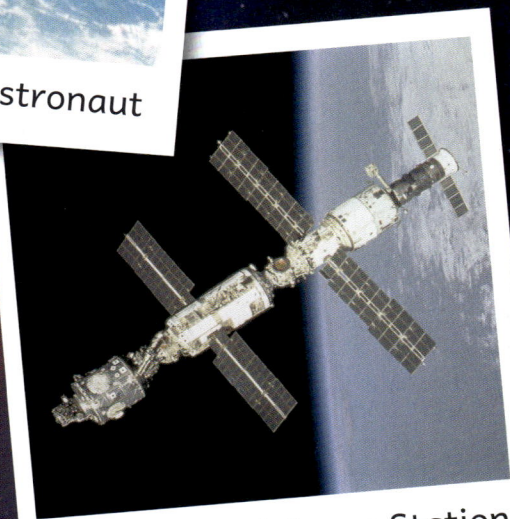

International Space Station

Quiz

1. What is the Sun?
a) A bright asteroid
b) A dwarf star
c) A giant star

2. What are the four solid planets closest to the Sun called?
a) Terrific planets
b) Tougher planets
c) Terrestrial planets

3. What is this called?

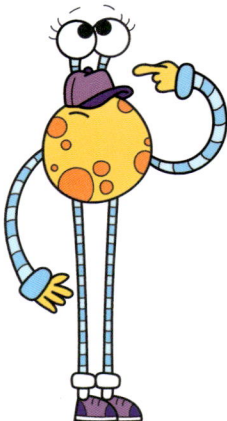

4. Uranus is...

a) An ice giant

b) A gas giant

c) A moon

5. What is the weather like on Neptune?

a) Wet

b) Hot

c) Windy

6. What is Voyager 1 carrying?

a) Plants

b) People

c) A golden disk

Turn over for answers

Index/Glossary

Alien pg 24
Life from another planet/somewhere other than Earth.

Dwarf planets pg 7, 15, 25
Dwarf planets have less gravity than regular planets. Their gravity is not strong enough to clear the surrounding area of space.

Dwarf star pg 8
A relatively small star which isn't as bright as others.

Gravity pg 9, 17
Gravity is a force that draws objects towards its centre. It's also why things fall to the ground.

The Milky Way pg 6
The spiral galaxy containing our solar system.

Moons pg 7, 12, 14, 17, 19, 21-22, 25
Natural satellites orbiting a planet/dwarf planet/asteroid.

NASA pg 24

The National Aeronautics and Space Administration (established in 1958) is in charge of the American civilian space program, and carries out aeronautics and aerospace research.

Orbit pg 9-12

An orbit is a repeating path that an object in space takes around another.

Planetary system pg 6

A group of planets or asteroids that orbit one or more stars.

Satellite pg 26

A small object that orbits a larger object in space. Satellites can be natural or man-made. For example, Earth's Moon is a natural satellite, and the International Space Station is a man-made satellite.

Book Bands for Guided Reading

The Institute of Education book banding system is a scale of colours that reflects the various levels of reading difficulty. The bands are assigned by taking into account the content, the language style, the layout and phonics. Word, phrase and sentence level work is also taken into consideration.

Maverick Early Readers are a bright, attractive range of books covering the pink to white bands. All of these books have been book banded for guided reading to the industry standard and edited by a leading educational consultant.

Fiction

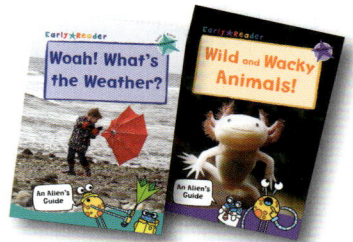

Non-fiction

To view the whole Maverick Readers scheme, visit our website at

www.maverickearlyreaders.com

Or scan the QR code above to view our scheme instantly!